WHEN DADDY SAYS GOODNIGHT TO THE STARS

By: Erik Usher

This book is dedicated to all the families of those First responders who selflessly spend nights away from their families to help yours.

More importantly, this is for my wonderful wife who had to answer this questions to our two children Maya and Max!

"When Daddy Says Goodnight to The Stars"
Copyright © 2024 by Erik Usher

All rights reserved. No part of this publication may be reproduced or transmitted in any form or by any means, electronic or mechanical, Including photocopying, recording or any information storage and retrieval system, without written permission from the copyright owner.

"Why isn't Daddy home tonight?" asked Max, hugging his favorite stuffed dog tightly. The soft glow of his bedside lamp lit up the room as he gazed at Mommy with curious eyes.

"Well, Max," said Mom, tucking him in, "Daddy is out helping people tonight. He's a Police Officer, and that means he's always ready to protect people when they're in trouble."

"Is Daddy chasing bad guys?" Max asked, his eyes wide.

"Sometimes," Mom said with a nod. "But mostly, Daddy is helping people—like finding someone who's lost or making sure everyone gets home safely."

"Does Daddy ever get scared?" Max whispered.

"Sometimes," Mom said softly. "But Daddy is very brave. He has special training to stay calm and make the right choices, even when things are hard."

"Does Daddy think about me when he's at work?" Max asked.

"Always," said Mom. "He says you're his little spark of courage. Thinking of you makes him brave, even on the toughest nights."

"But why does he have to work at night?"

"Because some people need help most when the world is quiet and asleep," Mom explained. "Daddy works so that other families can feel safe, just like you do here at home."

"Will he come home soon?" Max asked as he yawned.

"Yes, sweetheart," Mom said, pulling the blanket snug around him. "And when he does, he'll be so happy to see you. He loves hearing about your dreams."

That night, Max dreamed of his dad driving his police car under the stars, helping people stay safe. Even though he wasn't home, he knew he was a hero, and the stars were watching over both of them.

Pictures of my Dad

Pictures of me and my Dad

Drawings of my Dad

My favorite things about my Dad

Drawings of my Dad at work

Drawings of Mom and Dad

Drawings of Mom tucking me in

My favorite things about my Mom

www.ingramcontent.com/pod-product-compliance
Lightning Source LLC
Chambersburg PA
CBRC090840010526
44119CB00045B/500